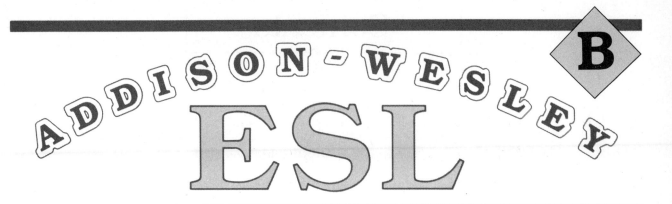

ADDISON-WESLEY ESL **B**

ACTIVITY BOOK

Michael Walker

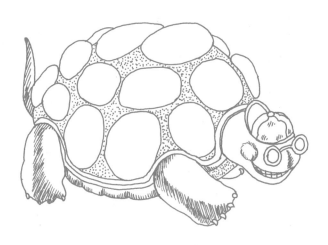

Addison-Wesley Publishing Company

Reading, Massachusetts • Menlo Park, California • New York • Don Mills, Ontario
Wokingham, England • Amsterdam • Bonn • Sydney • Singapore • Tokyo • Madrid • San Juan

Contents

Featuring EARLY LITERACY: Matching sentences to pictures 6, 8, 33, 44, 46 ◆ Following oral directions 4, 17, 18, 42 ◆ Comparing and contrasting 20, 32, 63 ◆ Getting information from pictures 16, 17, 23, 28 ◆◆ READING SKILLS (Decoding): Sound/letter 10, 22, 34, 48, 60, 73 ◆◆ READING SKILLS (Comprehension): Main idea 35 ◆ Details 50, 74 ◆ Making inferences 53, 61 ◆ Classifying 40-41, 54-55, 62, 66-67, 75 ◆ Understanding sequence 3, 20, 21, 25, 30, 49 ◆◆ WRITING SKILLS: Complete sentences 43, 45, 56, 57, 68, 71 ◆ Negative sentences 47, 71 ◆ Answers to questions 45, 47 ◆ Language experience 5, 7, 9, 17, 19, 56, 57 ◆◆ CONTENT AREA (Math): Number words 4 ◆ Math problems 12, 14, 76 ◆ Adding 12, 13 ◆ Subtracting 24, 51, 76 ◆ Telling time 7, 12, 24 ◆ Calculating time 50 ◆◆ PREPARATION FOR STANDARDIZED TESTING: 15, 27, 39, 53, 65, 78 ◆◆ STRUCTURES: Is/are, was/were 32 ◆ Before/after 29 ◆ Present tense 28 ◆ Simple past tense 28, 69, 70 ◆ Irregular past tense 71, 72 ◆ Object pronouns 19

A Publication of the World Language Division

Project Director: Elinor Chamas

Editorial Development: Margaret Grant

Production/Manufacturing: James W. Gibbons

Design, Art Direction, and Production: Taurins Design Associates, New York

Cover Art: John Sandford

Illustrators: Teresa Anderko 10, 12, 13, 18, 22, 30, 36, 47, 60, 63, 76; Ellen Appleby 34, 40, 41, 45, 50, 54, 55, 56, 61, 66, 67, 73, 79; Deborah Kaplan 3; Linda Knox 24, 26, 28, 39, 43, 46, 69; Ben Mahan 4, 11, 15, 32, 71, 74; Diane Paterson 33, 44, 48, 52, 58, 68; Meryl Henderson 6, 16, 20, 23, 27, 37, 49, 51, 57, 70, 78; Debbie Pinkney 8, 17, 21, 25, 72

ISBN 0-201-57814-X

3 4 5 6 7 8 9 10-WC-95 94 93 92

Follow the dots.

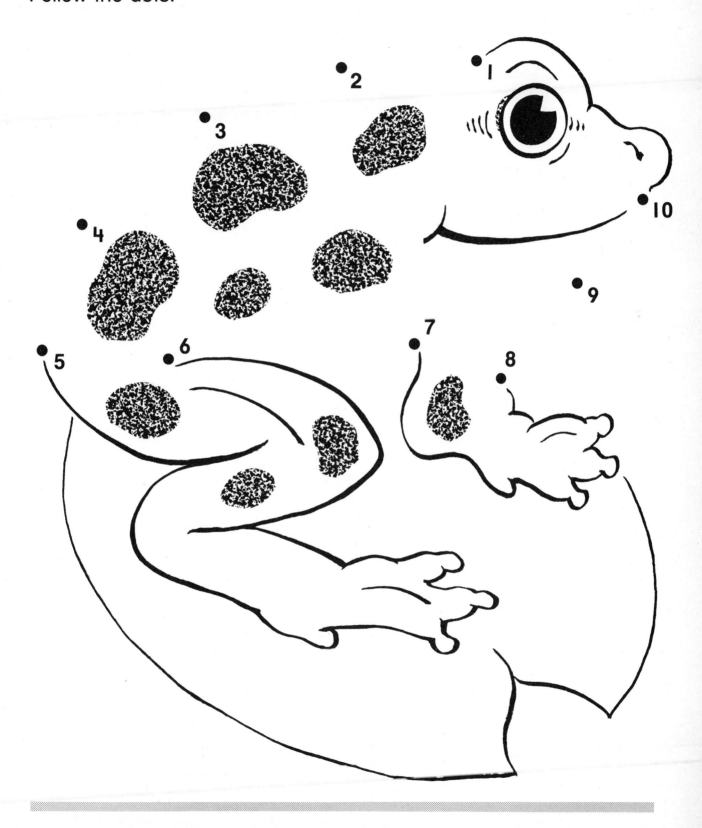

(After Level B, student page 5) **Recognizing numbers and sequence; developing hand/eye, fine motor skills coordination.** Students create a frog by following the dots from one to ten. Then they color the frog any color they wish.

3

Listen and follow directions.

(After Level B, student page 5) **Following oral directions; reviewing colors; reading number words.** First, students volunteer to read the numbers on the objects in the big picture. Then say, *What is number one?* (a bird). *Color the bird red.* Continue with each number, directing students to color the grass green, the sky blue, the flowers yellow, the tree brown, and the bus orange.

All About Me

1. My name is _____ .

2. I am _____ years old.

3. My hair is _____ .

4. My eyes are _____ .

A Picture of Me

(After Level B, student page 9) **Language experience.** Students work alone to fill in the answers to items 1 through 4. They draw themselves in colorful clothes in the space provided. Then they exchange papers and tell about one another (Substitute *her/his* for *my*.)

5

Find the matching picture.
Write the missing word.

_c_ 1. My ___little___ ___brother___ is sleeping.

___ 2. My _____ _____ is taking a shower.

___ 3. My _____ and _____ are getting dressed.

___ 4. My _____ _____ is eating.

___ 5. My _____ _____ is packing my lunch.

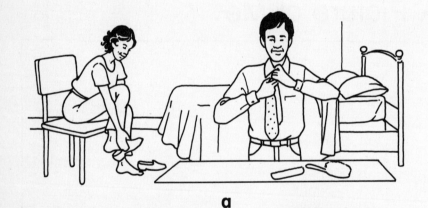

a

b

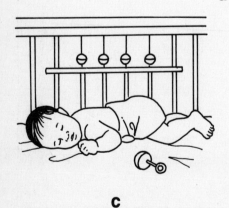

c

d

e

(After Level B, student page 11) **Matching sentences to pictures; reviewing family vocabulary.** Students match each sentence with a corresponding picture. They put the letter of the correct picture on the line provided and write the correct word(s) in the space(s) provided. After completion, model questions, such as *Who is (sleep)ing?*, and have volunteers read their answers aloud.

6

What Time Is It?

1. It's __seven__ o'clock.

It's time to get up.

2. It's _____ o'clock.

It's time for breakfast.

3. It's _____ o'clock.

It's time for recess.

4. It's _____ o'clock.

It's time for lunch.

5. It's _____ o'clock.

It's time to go home.

6. It's _____ o'clock.

It's time for dinner.

(After Level B, student page 13) **Telling time; language experience.** Students write in the correct number word for the time in each item. Then they take turns asking and answering time questions, e.g., *What time is it? It's seven o'clock.*

Find the matching picture.

_____ 1. I want to ride my bike.   _____ 2. I want to play ball.

_____ 3. I want to jump rope.   _____ 4. I want to draw.

_____ 5. I want to read.   _____ 6. I want to roller-skate.

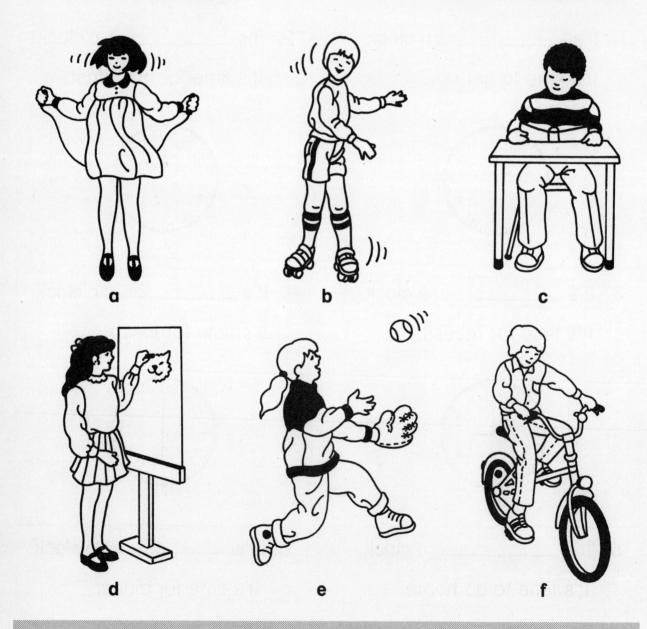

a   b   c

d   e   f

(After Level B, student page 14) **Matching sentences with pictures.** Students read each sentence, match it with the corresponding picture, and write the letter of the picture in the space provided.

What can you do?
Circle **I can** or **I can't.**

1. I can
   I can't
   ride a bike.

2. I can
   I can't
   play the piano.

3. I can
   I can't
   ice skate.

4. I can
   I can't
   ride a horse.

5. I can
   I can't
   play soccer.

6. I can
   I can't
   swim.

Finish the sentence any way you like.
Draw a picture.

I can _____ .

I can't _____ .

(After Level B, student page 15) **Expressing ability and inability; language experience.** Students read each sentence and circle *I can* or *I can't,* according to their own abilities. Then they draw a picture of one other thing they *can* do and a picture of something they *can't* but want to learn how to do, and complete the sentences. You may need to help them with this. Allow time for volunteers to read sentences aloud.

Say the word.
Write the **first** letter you hear.

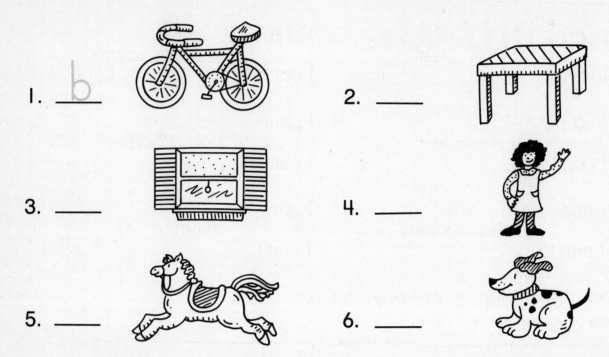

1. b

2. ___

3. ___

4. ___

5. ___

6. ___

Say the word.
Write the **last** letter you hear.

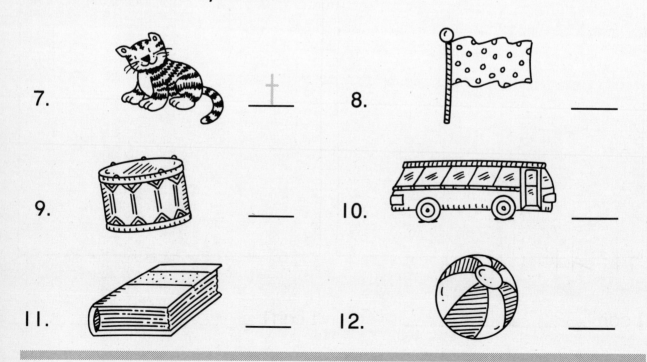

7. t

8. ___

9. ___

10. ___

11. ___

12. ___

(After Level B, student page 16) **Identifying/writing initial consonants; identifying/writing final consonants.**
Students identify each picture. They write the initial consonant in the space provided for items 1–6 and the final consonant for items 7–12.

10

Read and follow directions.

1. Color the school bus yellow.

2. Draw a bird in the tree.

3. Draw four flowers under the tree.

4. Draw a book on the table.

5. Draw a boy next to the desk.

6. Color the chalkboard green.

(After Level B, student page 17) **Following written directions; reviewing in, on, under, next to.** First, students familiarize themselves with the illustration. Then they read each item in the directions, doing what it says before going on to the next item. After they have followed the directions for all six items, students ask each other questions, e.g., *What color is the bus?* to check each item.

Find the matching clock.

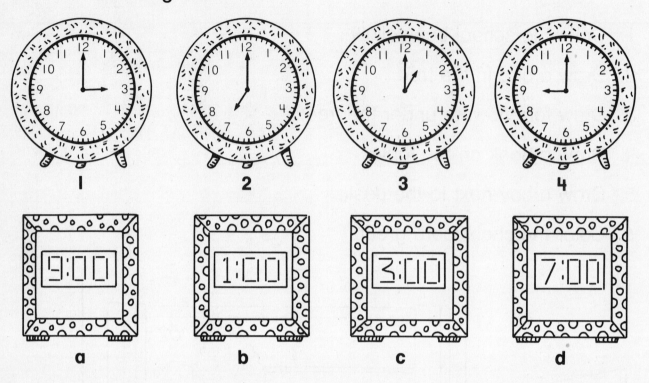

Circle the correct clock.

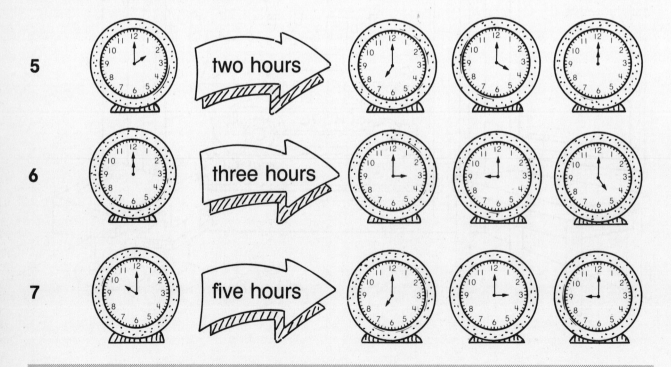

5 two hours

6 three hours

7 five hours

(After Level B, student page 18) **Telling time; problem solving with addition.** Students match the traditional clocks and digital clocks at the top of the page. Then they circle the clock that gives the correct time after *two*, *three* and *five* hours have passed. Discuss fully.

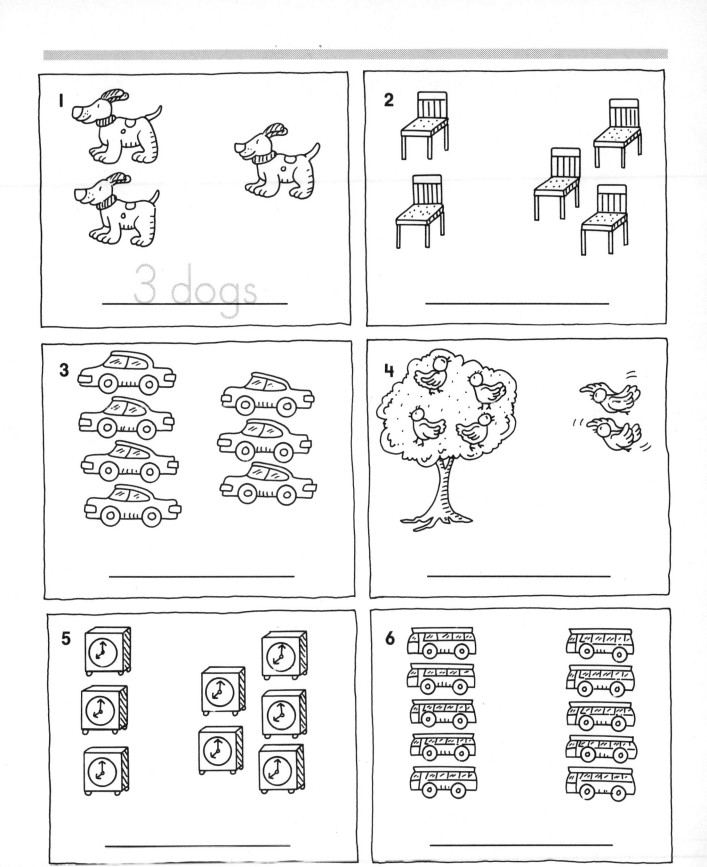

1. 3 dogs

2. _____

3. _____

4. _____

5. _____

6. _____

(After Level B, student page 19) **Math; adding; spelling.** Students add up the objects in each box and write the number and the object name on the rule provided, e.g., the answer for number 1. would be *3 dogs*. Discuss the answers with the whole group to make sure that everyone understood how to add up the objects.

13

Read the sentences. Write the missing word.

1. Once there was a little _____ hen.

      red   bed   read

2. "Who will help me _____ the wheat?" she asked.

      play   ride   plant

3. "Not I," said the duck, the cat, and the _____.

      dog   frog   bird

4. "Who will help me _____ the bread?" she asked.

      plant   feed   eat

5. "I _____ !" said the duck, the cat, and the dog.

      do   am   will

6. "No you _____ ." said the Little Red Hen.

      won't   will   can't

7. "I _____ it myself and I'll eat it myself," she said.

      made   packed   talked

(After Level B, student pages 21–23) **Developing basic sight word vocabulary; using words in context.**
Students circle and copy the correct word to complete each sentence. Check orally; give each student a chance
to read aloud.

14

Read the word.
Find the picture.

1 car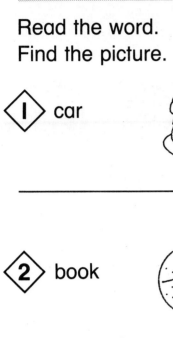

2 book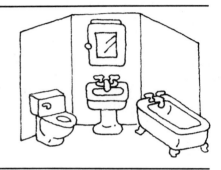

3 boys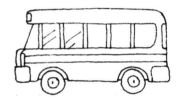

4 pencil

5 window

(After Level B, student Unit 1) **Preparation for standardized testing.** Students look at the example and read the word *car*. Then they note that the picture of the car has been marked with an X. Students work independently after the example is discussed. After completion, have students identify each picture. Encourage the use of full sentences.

15

Look at the picture. Read the sentence.
Check **YES** or **NO**.

	YES	NO
1. The principal is in the office.		
2. The librarian is eating.		
3. They are singing.		
4. He is reading.		
5. The nurse is in the hall.		
6. The teacher is writing.		

(After Level B, student page 25) **Getting information from pictures; reading for details.** Students look at each picture, read the corresponding sentence, and then check **YES** if the sentence is true, **NO** if it is not true. Discuss orally when completed.

Look at the picture.
Answer the questions.

1. How many brothers does she have?

   She has _____ .

2. How many cats does she have?

   She has _____ .

3. How many dogs does she have?

   She has _____ .

Draw a picture of your family.
Then write about your family.

My Family

I have _____

_____

(After Level B, student page 26) **Following oral instructions; getting information from pictures; language experience.** Have students color one dog *red* and one dog *yellow.* The cats should be colored *black, gray* and *brown.* Students answer questions about the picture. They then draw a picture of their own family on a separate piece of paper and write sentences about family members and pets.

CROSSWORD PUZZLE

Across		Down	
3	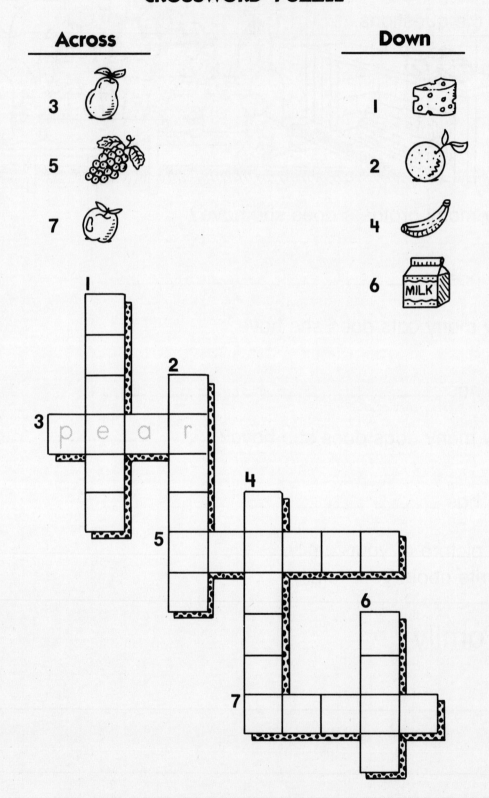	1	
5		2	
7		4	
		6	MILK

(After Level B, student page 27) **Spelling; following directions.** Work with the class, having students name the picture under *Across 3* and find the word *pear* in the puzzle. Point out that only one letter goes in each box. Have students work in pairs or independently to complete the puzzle.

Read the sentences.
Write the missing word.

me   you   him   her   us   them

1. I am making lemonade.

   Can you help _____ ?

2. Bill is fixing his bike.

   Can you help _____ ?

3. Jill is making cookies.

   Can you help _____ ?

4. They are washing their dog.

   Can you help _____ ?

5. You are feeding the dog.

   Can I help _____ ?

6. We are making juice.

   Can you help _____ ?

When do you need help?
Draw a picture.
Then finish the sentences.

I am _____ .

Can you help _____?

(After Level B, student page 29) **Completing sentences using object pronouns; language experience.**
Students complete *Can you help* _____ ? questions using the pronouns listed at the top of the page.
Then volunteers answer each item. Then, they draw a picture of themselves performing an activity they may
need help with.

Read the words. Look at the pictures.
Put the pictures in the correct order.
Write the letters on the lines.

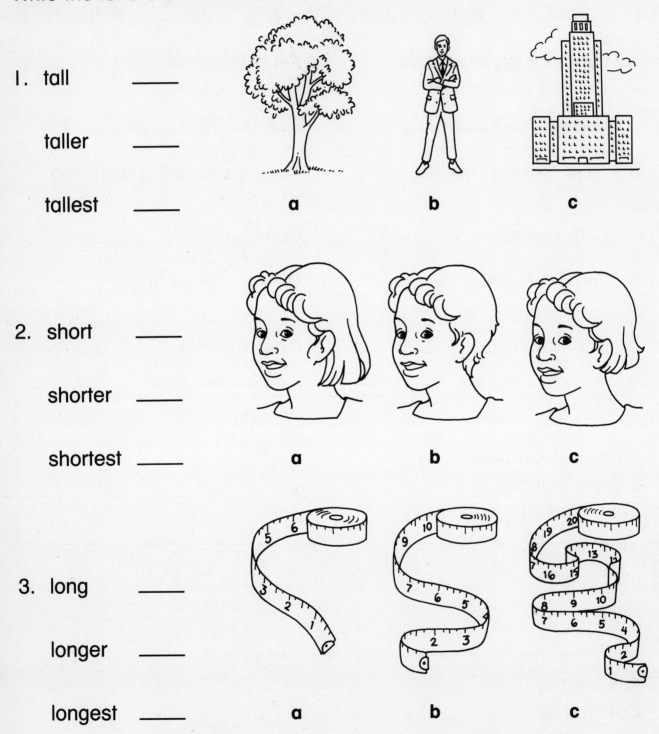

1. tall   _____

    taller   _____

    tallest   _____

        a   b   c

2. short   _____

    shorter   _____

    shortest   _____

        a   b   c

3. long   _____

    longer   _____

    longest   _____

        a   b   c

(After Level B, student page 30) **Comparing and contrasting; sequencing.** Students read the three comparative adjectives in each item, match them with the corresponding picture, and write the letter of the picture next to each adjective. After completion, discuss fully. Can students identify the pictures and create full sentences about them?

What happens first? Write 1.
What happens next? Write 2.
What happens last? Write 3.

a.

b.

c.

(After Level B, student page 31) **Sequencing.** Students look at the three pictures in each row and number the boxes in the correct order. Follow-up: Students furnish the art work for a story sequence. They mix up the sequence and ask a partner to decide the correct order. Encourage volunteers to "tell the stores," e.g., *First you get up. Then you brush your teeth. Then you go to school.*

21

Cut out the pictures at the bottom of the page.
Read the words.
Find the picture that begins with the same sound.

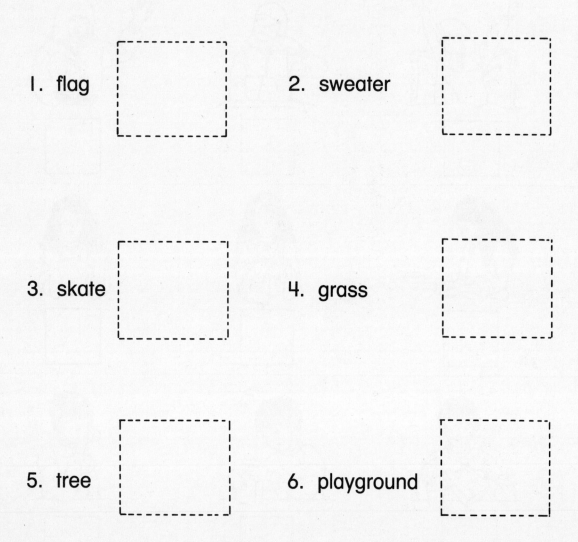

1. flag

2. sweater

3. skate

4. grass

5. tree

6. playground

(After Level B, student page 32) **Recognizing initial blends.** Students cut out the pictures at the bottom of the page and paste each one next to the word that begins with the same initial blend.

Look at the picture. Read the sentences.
Write the missing word.

1. The first student in line has some _____ juice _____ .

   milk   grapes   (juice)

2. The _____ student in line has an apple.

   first   second   third

3. The girl at the table is eating _____ .

   an apple   a banana   a sandwich

4. The boy at the table is eating _____ .

   grapes   an orange   some cheese

(After Level B, student page 33) **Getting information from an illustration; understanding ordinals; identifying food.** Students look over the picture for a minute or two. Then they work in pairs to circle and write the correct word(s). Then the whole class goes over each item together, with volunteers providing the answers. Finally, ask students what else they can tell you about the picture.

Look at the two clocks. How long did it take?
Circle the answer.

1.

two hours   three hours   four hours

2.

two hours   three hours   four hours

Draw a picture of you doing something.
Then finish the clocks.
Show when you started and when you finished.

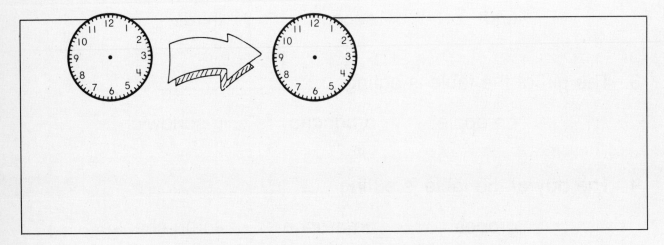

(After Level B, student page 34) **Telling time; problem solving with subtraction.** Students decide how long
each activity took and circle the number of hours. Then volunteers tell what happened in each picture and
how long it took. After they have drawn themselves, they give the page to a partner who describes their activity
and tells how long it took.

Who won the race?
Write the names.

1. Sara: 10 minutes   FIRST   SECOND   THIRD

   Joe: 8 minutes

   Jean: 4 minutes   Jean   _____   _____

2. Bill: 6 minutes   FIRST   SECOND   THIRD

   Al: 7 minutes

   Maria: 8 minutes   _____   _____   _____

3. Jesse: 2 minutes   FIRST   SECOND   THIRD

   Ana: 1 minute

   Luis: 3 minutes   _____   _____   _____

(After Level B, student page 34) **Identifying sequence.** Look at the first item with your students. Model the story for the first item. Help students to understand that Sara ran the race in ten minutes, Joe ran it in eight minutes and Jean ran it in four minutes. Ask who came in *first, second* and *third*. Volunteers can answer orally. Then students write the correct name under *First, Second,* and *Third.*

Help the tortoise race to the river.

(After Level B, student pages 37–39) **Developing fine motor skills; visual discrimination; describing a sequence.** Students find their way through the maze. After completion, volunteers tell what they found along the way.

Read the sentence.
Find the matching picture.

 He's crying.

 She's eating lunch.

3 She's fixing the sink.

 I have two brothers.

 She's brushing her teeth.

(After Level B, Unit 2) **Preparation for standardized testing.** Students will work independently after the first item is discussed. Establish that they are to read the sentence, look at the pictures, and put an X on the picture that matches the sentence.

Look at the pictures. Finish the sentence.

1. My father was in the _bathroom_.

He was taking a shower.

He was brushing his teeth.

He is in the _____ now.

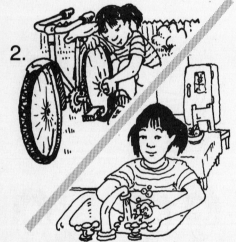

2. My sister was in the _____.

She was fixing her bike.

She was washing the car.

She is in the _____ now.

3. I was on the _____.

I was sweeping.

I was reading.

I am in the _____ now.

(After Level B, student page 41) **Getting information from pictures; comparing simple past, past progressive and present tense.** Students circle one phrase and write one correct word in the blank for each item. Remind students to pay careful attention to *was* (past) and *is/am* (present). Have volunteers read the items aloud. Discuss with students how they used the pictures to help them choose their answers.

Write the missing word.

1. The first day of the week is _____ .

2. The day before Saturday is _____ .

3. The day after Wednesday is _____ .

4. The second day of the week is _____ .

Finish the sentences any way you like.
Draw a picture.

On Saturday, I like to _____ .

On Sunday, I like to _____ .

(After Level B, student page 42) **Recognizing days of the week; *before*/*after*; ordinals; language experience.**
Let students work with their textbooks open as they complete the sentences.

29

Write the months.

REBVEMON

NUJE

RILAP

SUGATU

RANUJAY

BUYRAREF

YAM

LUJY

BECEDREM

RECOTOB

RACMH

PETESMREB

1. _____

2. _____

3. _____

4. _____

5. _____

6. _____

7. _____

8. _____

9. _____

10. _____

11. November

12. _____

(After Level B, student page 43) **Spelling; sequencing the months of the year.** Students unscramble the letters to spell the months of the year. Then they write the months in correct order on the lines provided.

	1	2	3	4	5	6	7	8	9	10
January										
February										
March										
April										
May										
June										
July										
August										
September										
October										
November										
December										

(After Level B, student page 43) **Counting; recording information on a bar graph.** As a volunteer calls out the names of the months, students indicate by a show of hands if it is their birthday month. Then they record the number of birthdays on the graph by coloring in the correct number of squares. Finally, they ask each other questions, e.g., *How many birthdays are there in January? Are there more birthdays in June or July?*

Look at the pictures. Finish the sentences.

1. How many elephants were there in the morning?

   There   was   one _____ .
           were

2. How many bears are there now?

   There   is   _____ .
           are

3. How many dolls were there in the morning?

   There _____ .

4. How many elephants are there now?

   There _____ .

5. _____ two dolls now.

(After Level B, student page 45) **Comparing and contrasting; completing sentences with *is*/*are*; *was*/*were*.**
Students circle or write the verb and complete the rest of the sentence. Discuss fully after completion and have
pairs read each question and answer it aloud.

Find the matching picture.

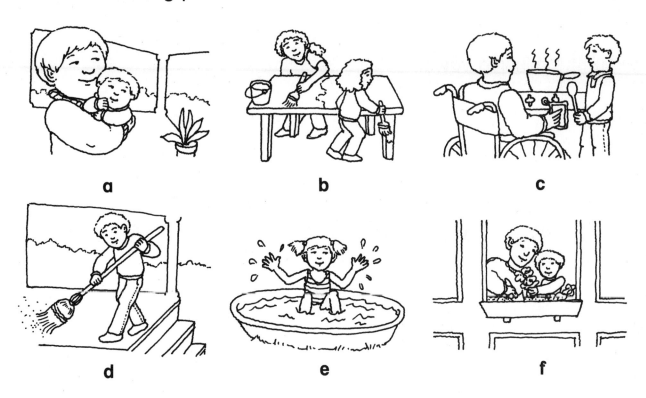

a   b   c

d   e   f

_____ 1. He was taking care of the baby.

_____ 2. They were planting flowers.

_____ 3. They were painting.

_____ 4. They were cooking.

_____ 5. She was playing in the pool.

_____ 6. He was sweeping the porch.

van   red   big   frog   lunch

Write the missing vowel.

1. b __a__ g

2. cl ___ ck

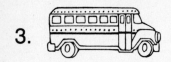

3. b ___ s

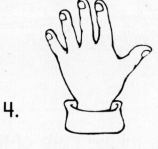

4. h ___ nd

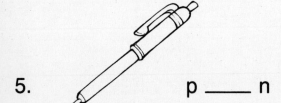

5. p ___ n

6. c ___ t

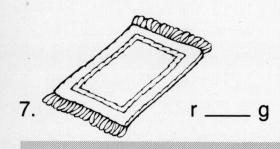

7. r ___ g

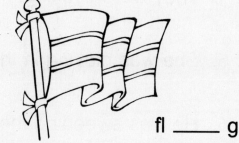

8. fl ___ g

(After Level B, student page 48) **Discriminating among medial short vowel sounds.** Students volunteer to read the sample words. Then they work on their own to complete the word label for each picture.

Last Saturday, my family was very busy. Luis and Linda were cleaning their bedrooms. Mom and Dad were washing windows. Ralph, my cat, was busy, too. He was washing his face. I was taking care of my baby sister.

What is the main idea of the story?

◯ The brother and sister were cleaning their bedrooms.

◯ The family was very busy last Saturday.

◯ The cat was washing his face.

Draw what Mom and Dad were doing.

(After Level B, student page 49) **Recognizing main idea; illustrating a story.** Discuss the concept of main idea before students read the paragraph. Then students read silently, fill in the oval before the sentence that states the main idea and draw a picture illustrating what Mom and Dad were doing.

35

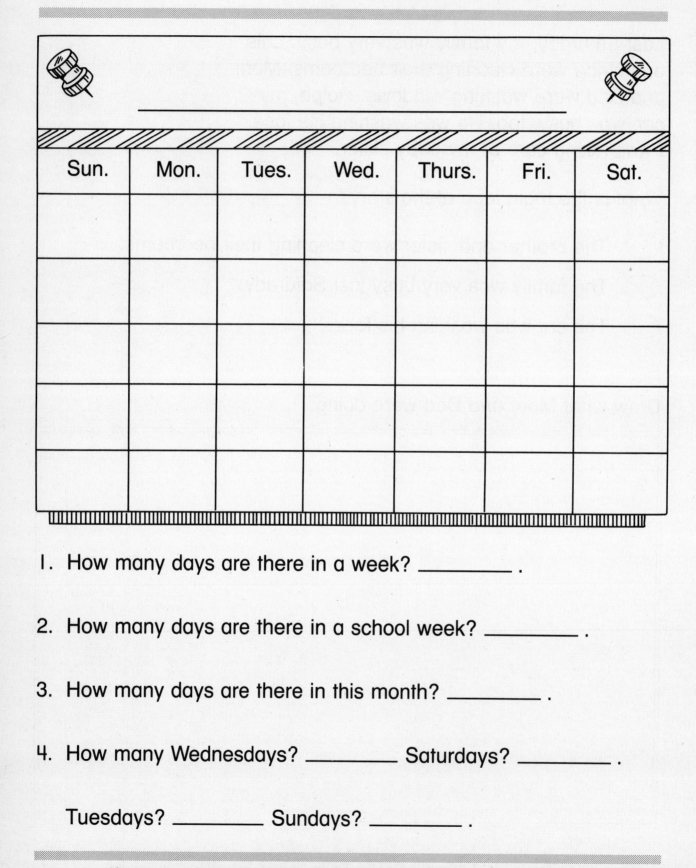

Sun.	Mon.	Tues.	Wed.	Thurs.	Fri.	Sat.

1. How many days are there in a week? _____ .

2. How many days are there in a school week? _____ .

3. How many days are there in this month? _____ .

4. How many Wednesdays? _____ Saturdays? _____ .

Tuesdays? _____ Sundays? _____ .

(After Level B, student page 50) **Making a calendar; identifying the days of the week; counting.** Students fill in the name of the present month at the top of the calendar; then they fill in the numbers of the days for the whole month. They should fill in all holidays and their own special days (birthday, school trip, etc.). Then they answer the questions orally and write the number answers in the space provided.

36

Tell the math story. How much money do they have?

1. TOTAL $1.15

2. TOTAL _____

3. TOTAL _____

4. TOTAL _____

(After Level B, student page 51) **Identifying/counting money.** Read the direction line at the top of the page.
Ask students to tell what they see in the first picture. Then ask them to count the money out loud (one dollar,
ten, fifteen, one dollar fifteen). Students should write the total in numbers with a dollar sign for each frame.

37

Draw a beautiful forest.   Draw Anansi.

Draw great flowers.   Draw the moon in the sky.

Draw wonderful trees.   Write about your picture.

(After Level B, student pages 54–57) **Following written directions; creative expression.** Students draw and describe their scenes. Students may write on a separate piece of paper or in the art space. Help less capable students by letting them dictate their sentences to you.

Fill in the oval next to the sentence
that describes the picture.

1. ○ She's taking a bath.

   ○ She's taking a nap.

   ○ She's in the living room.

2. ○ She's parking the car on the street.

   ○ She's washing the car.

   ○ She's putting the car in the garage.

3. ○ He's sweeping the yard.

   ○ He's sweeping the steps.

   ○ He's washing the steps.

4. ○ They're at baseball practice.

   ○ They're at the zoo.

   ○ They're at soccer practice.

(After Level B, student Unit 3) **Preparation for standardized testing.** Students look at each picture and read
the three sentence choices. Then they fill in the oval next to the sentence that best states what the picture
shows.

(After Level B, student pages 58–59) **Classifying; identifying occupations.** Students cut out the pieces of art at the top of page 79 and paste the workers where they belong in this scene. Then they should ask and answer information questions, e.g., *Who is this? Where is he? What is the (mail carrier) doing?* You may wish to give TPR commands, e.g., *Put the mail carrier by/at the mailbox*, etc.

CROSSWORD PUZZLE

Across

1. A mail carrier _____ the mail.
6. A trash collector _____ trash.
7. A _____ reports the news.
8. A _____ serves people their food.

Down

2. A _____ types letters.
3. A clerk _____ in a store.
4. A _____ works in a hospital.
5. A baseball _____ plays baseball.

(After Level B, student page 60) **Completing sentences; describing occupations; spelling; following directions.** Students read the first item ACROSS. One student gives the answer: *delivers*. Students write the word *delivers*, one letter to a box, in the puzzle. They continue with other items in the same way.

Write the sentences.

1. sell

She doesn't sell shoes.

She sells apples.

2. cut

She _____

_____

3. drive

They _____

_____

4. play

He _____

_____

5. deliver

They _____

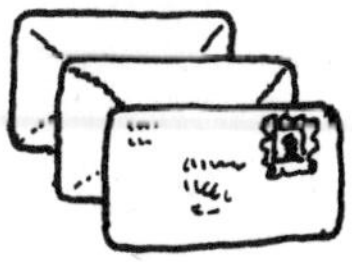

_____

(After Level B, student page 61) **Writing complete sentences.** Students write two complete sentences in the simple present, negative and affirmative, based on the illustrations for each item.

Find the matching picture.

a   b   c   d

e   f   g   h

___g___ 1. It chases the bird.

_____ 2. The baby kisses the dog.

_____ 3. The boy watches the football game.

_____ 4. It chases the mail carrier.

_____ 5. He catches the football.

_____ 6. She kisses the baby.

_____ 7. It catches the stick.

_____ 8. The dog watches TV.

(After Level B, student page 62) **Matching sentences and pictures.** Students read the sentences and match them with the appropriate pictures. They write the letter of the picture beside the sentence it goes with.

Answer the questions.

1. When does she get up?

She gets up at 7:00.

2. What does she wash?

_____

3. What does she make for lunch?

_____

4. Who does she kiss?

_____

5. What does she catch?

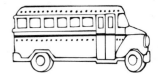

_____

6. When does she get to school?

_____

7. Where does she play before school?

_____

(After Level B, student page 63) **Writing sentences to answer simple present tense questions.** Students write complete sentences to answer the questions, using the pictures on the right as cues. Discuss fully after completion; check for s/es endings on the verbs.

45

Find the matching picture.

a   b   c   d

e   f   g   h

_____ 1. He has a hammer.

_____ 2. She has a horse.

_____ 3. It has a stick.

_____ 4. He has a paintbrush.

_____ 5. She has a ladder.

_____ 6. It has a ball.

_____ 7. She has a tractor.

_____ 8. He has a hammer and a saw.

(After Level B, student page 64) **Matching sentences and pictures.** Students read each sentence and match it to the appropriate illustration. They write the letter of the illustration beside the sentence it goes with.

Answer the questions.

1. Does he have a cat?

<u>No, he doesn't. He has a dog.</u>

2. Does he have a paintbrush?

_____

3. Does she have a ruler?

_____

4. Does he have a wagon?

_____

5. Does she have some grapes?

_____

6. Does he have some cookies?

_____

(After Level B, student page 65) **Writing negative answers to questions; adding correct information.** Students write two sentences in response to each question, using the example as a model.

47

Circle the word that has the same long vowel sound as the picture.

1. knife   cake   toes

2. tree   grapes   cat

3. grapes   nose   truck

4. cheese   bed   plane

(After Level B, student page 66) **Discriminating among long vowels.** Model the key words and all other words if necessary. After completion, you might have students illustrate and label three or four words of their choice on a separate piece of paper. Pairs can exchange papers and read them aloud.

The sentences in these stories are not in the correct order. Write numbers 1, 2, and 3 to show the correct order.

_____ He starts work at seven o'clock.

_____ The mail carrier gets up at six o'clock.

_____ He always delivers the mail to our house at twelve o'clock.

_____ She brings the stick back to me.

_____ My dog is very smart.

_____ She catches a stick when I throw it.

(After Level B, student page 67) **Sequencing.** Students read the sentences in their present order and decide what the correct order should be. Then they number the sentences in correct order.

49

Read the story. Answer the questions.

Tomorrow City Skating Rink will be open for ice-skating. Linda wants to be the first person on the ice tomorrow. She wants to get there at eight o'clock. One hour later, the Snack Bar will open. Linda can go there to buy hot chocolate and warm up.

1. What time does Linda want to get to

   City Skating Rink tomorrow? _____

2. How many hours later will the

   Snack Bar open? _____

3. What time will that be? _____

Linda gets everything she needs for tomorrow—her skates, coat, scarf and mittens. "Mom," calls Linda. "Can I have 1 quarter and 2 dimes to buy hot chocolate tomorrow?" "Sure," her mother says. "Here you are."

4. What coins did Linda ask for? _____

5. How much money was that? _____

(After Level B, student page 69) **Identifying details; calculating time; counting money.** Students read the story about City Skating Rink and answer the questions. Answers can be one or two words. Then the class discusses their answers and how they arrived at them.

How many are there now?
Tell the math story.

1. _____3 bikes_____

2. _____

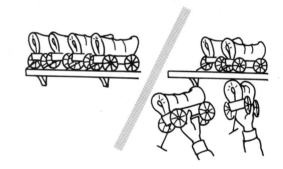

3. _____

4. _____

5. _____

6. _____

(After Level B, student page 69) **Math: subtracting.** Read the direction lines at the top of the page. Read the question and have a student give the answer orally. Students then write *3* or *3 bikes* on the line. Have students work in pairs, working out the subtraction and writing their answers in the book.

(After Level B, student pages 72–75) **Identifying and describing a sequence.** Students identify each stage of the apple chain and number the pictures accordingly. Encourage free oral description of the stages after completion.

Read the story. Then read the questions.
Choose the best answer.

Dr. Jackson is a very busy person. Every morning he goes to the hospital and visits sick people. He helps them a lot. He stays there three hours from 9:00 to 12:00. Then he eats lunch. After lunch, he goes to his office to see more sick people. He stays there until 5:00. Then he goes home, tired but happy.

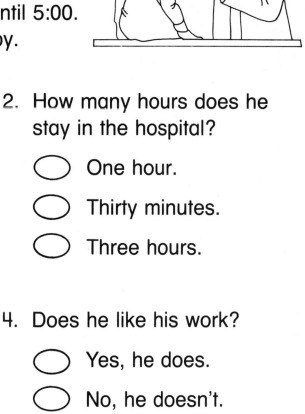

1. Where does Dr. Jackson work?

   ◯ In a hospital.

   ◯ In a bank.

   ◯ In a house.

2. How many hours does he stay in the hospital?

   ◯ One hour.

   ◯ Thirty minutes.

   ◯ Three hours.

3. What time does he go home?

   ◯ Three o'clock.

   ◯ Four o'clock.

   ◯ Five o'clock.

4. Does he like his work?

   ◯ Yes, he does.

   ◯ No, he doesn't.

   ◯ He never goes to work.

(After Level B, student Unit 4) **Identifying details; making inferences.** Students read the story and answer each question, filling in the ovals next to their choices.

53

(After Level B, student pages 76–77) **Classifying.** Students cut out the pieces of art in the middle of page 79 and paste the pictures where they belong in this scene. Then they should ask and answer questions using prepositions of place, e.g., *Where do you want to go? Why do you want to go there?* You may wish to give TPR commands, e.g., *Put the dolphins in the Water Show.*

What do they have to do every day?

1. _____

2. _____

3. _____

4. _____

5. _____

What do *you* have to do every day?

I have to _____ .

(After Level B, student page 79) **Writing complete sentences; expressing obligations; language experience.**
Students write one sentence for each picture, using *have to* or *has to*. Then they draw a picture showing
something they have to do every day and write a sentence describing it. You may need to help them to spell the
words in their sentence.

What are they going to do tomorrow?

1. _____

2. _____

3. _____

4. _____

5. _____

What are *you* going to do tomorrow?

I'm going to _____ .

(After Level B, student page 81) **Writing complete sentences; language experience.** Students work with a partner to write a sentence that describes each illustration. Sentences must use *going to* future. Then students draw a picture of something they are going to do and write a sentence about it.

57

Follow these directions.

1. The farmer is going to milk the cow.
   Draw the cow in the barn.

2. The farmer's son is going to drive
   the truck. Draw the son in the truck.
   Color the truck green.

3. The farmer's daughter is going to feed
   the pigs. Draw three more pigs in the pig pen.
   Color them pink.

(After Level B, student pages 82–83) **Following written directions.** Students read and follow written directions to complete the picture. Then they practice asking and answering information questions and *going to* questions, e.g., *Who's this? Where's the farmer? What's he going to do?*

Now plan a trip with your class. Discuss where
you could go. List a few possibilities.

_____   _____   _____

_____   _____   _____

_____   _____   _____

Now take a vote. Decide where you want to go.
Then write about your trip.

We're going to take _____.

We're going on _____.
                              (day)

We're going by _____.
                         (transportation)

We'll get to _____ at _____.

We're going to _____.

Then we'll _____.

It's going to be a _____ day!

(After Level B, student page 83) **Language experience; illustrating a story.** Students complete each sentence, creating a story about a real or imaginary class trip.

59

Circle the word that has the same
vowel sound as the picture.

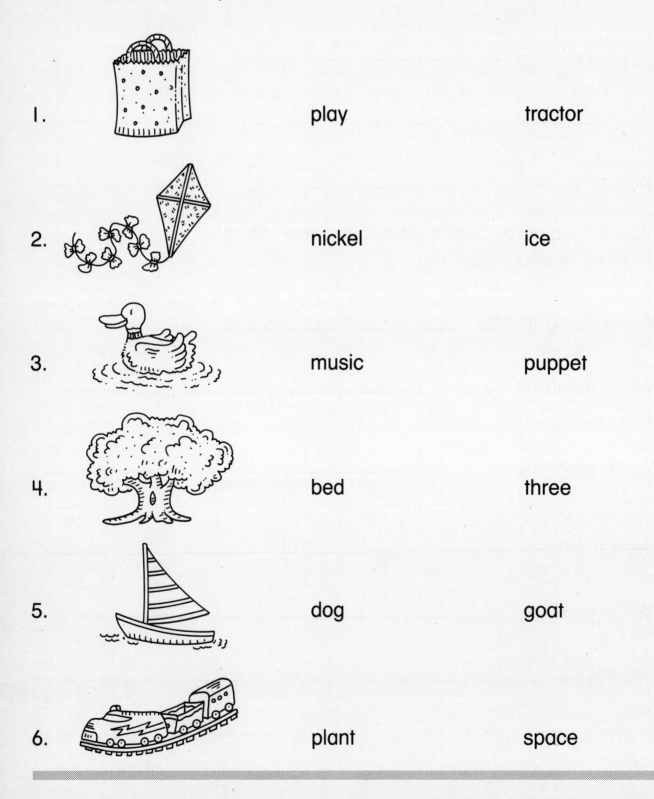

1. play   tractor

2. nickel   ice

3. music   puppet

4. bed   three

5. dog   goat

6. plant   space

(After Level B, student page 84) **Discriminating between long and short vowel sounds.** Students circle the
word on the right that has the same vowel sound as the pictured word.

Read the story. Then read the questions.
Choose the best answer.

Roberto was taking care of his baby brother Carlos. Carlos was playing in a small pool in the back yard. Carlos was very happy. He was playing with his toys. Suddenly, a big bee stung him on the finger. Carlos started to cry. Roberto jumped up and ran to Carlos.

1. What happened next?

   ◯ Roberto left the baby alone and chased the bee.

   ◯ Roberto picked up the baby and went to get his mother.

   ◯ Roberto's father came out to cut the grass.

2. How did Carlos feel?

   ◯ Happy

   ◯ Scared

   ◯ Hungry

3. How did Roberto feel?

   ◯ Sad

   ◯ Happy

   ◯ Tired

(After Level B, student page 85) **Making inferences.** Students read the story on their own and decide what will happen next. After everyone has finished, have someone read the paragraph aloud. Ask volunteers to give their answers and to explain how they chose these answers.

In the woods	On a farm	In the ocean

rabbit   bird   bear   deer

horse   cow   octopus   goat

hen   whale   dolphin   fish

(After Level B, student page 86) **Classifying.** Students decide where each of the animals live and they write the name of the animal in the appropriate column. They can add other animals they know as well.

Color the taller one blue.
Color the shorter one red.

1

2

3

Color the tallest one yellow.
Color the shortest one green.

4

5

6

(After Level B, student page 88) **Comparing and contrasting size.** Have students look at the two horses in item 1. Ask, *Which is taller? Which is shorter? Color the taller one blue. Color the shorter one red.* Students work in pairs to do the rest of the items in the first column. Then they compare the items in the right-hand column. After all the pictures are colored, students go over their answers together.

1. **ball**

   will

   all

   still

2. **name**

   game

   come

   home

3. **tail**

   seal

   feel

   whale

4. **cat**

   that

   boat

   late

5. **bad**

   made

   mad

   head

6. **talk**

   make

   walk

   take

7. **stand**

   pond

   feed

   hand

8. **kittens**

   kitchen

   mittens

   chickens

9. **zoo**

   go

   grow

   you

1. _____

2. _____

3. _____

4. _____

(After Level B, student pages 90–93) **Developing basic sight vocabulary; identifying rhyming words, using words in context.** Students circle the word in each item that rhymes with the bold-face word, then choose four words to use in sentences. Encourage your most capable students to write rhyming couplets or a 4-line poem.

Mark the correct word with an X.

1.   horse   van   rug   window

2.   brush   pony   bird   hand

3.   dollar   pet   tractor   doll

4.   boat   apple   pet   bike

5.   seal   lake   like   rope

6.   cent   milk   teeth   plane

7.   duck   rat   cake   head

(After Level B, Unit 5) **Preparation for standardized testing.** Tell students to find the word that has: 1) the same beginning sound as *wagon*, 2) the same beginning sound as *puzzle*, 3) the same end sound as *hall*, 4) the same vowel sound as *bag*, 5) the same vowel sound as *play*, 6) the same vowel sound as *cheese*, 7) rhymes with *truck*.

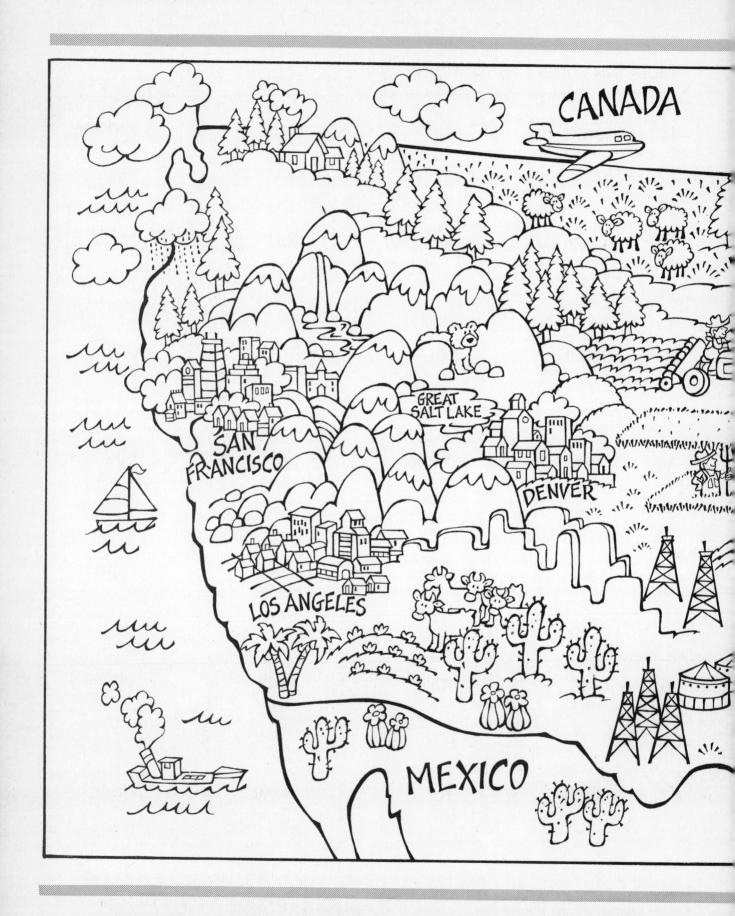

(After Level B, student pages 94–95) **Classifying.** Students cut out the pieces of art from the bottom of page 79 and place each item where it belongs on this map. Then they can talk about locations, e.g., *Where is the Washington Monument? It's here in Washington, D.C.*

Write the sentences.

1. laugh

She didn't laugh at the clown.
She laughed at a monkey.

2. park

He _____

_____

3. fix

They _____

_____

4. miss

He _____

_____

(After Level B, student page 96) **Writing complete sentences.** Students write a negative past tense sentence about the picture on the left and a positive sentence about the picture on the right. As sentences are read aloud after completion, stress the -t end sound of these past tense verbs.

Look at the picture.
Write the missing word in the sentence.

1. walk

2. pick

3. chase

4. fix

5. brush

6. cook

This is what a farm family did last Saturday.

1. In the morning, Grandpa _____walked_____ in the woods.

2. Judy and Tom _____ strawberries.

3. The baby _____ the chickens out in the yard.

4. Mom and Dad _____ the fence near the barn.

5. Jean and Patrick _____ the horses.

6. At 6:00 Grandma and Grandpa _____ chicken on the grill.

(After Level B, student page 97) **Constructing simple past tense; completing sentences.** Students complete
the story by looking at the appropriate illustration for that item and writing the past tense of the given verb
in the blank provided.

69

Look at the picture.
Write the missing word in the sentence.

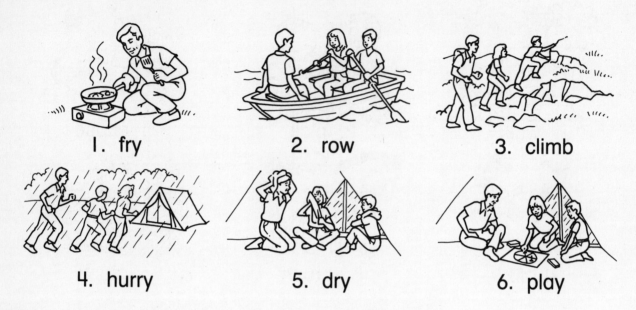

1. fry   2. row   3. climb

4. hurry   5. dry   6. play

This is what a father and his son and daughter
did last weekend. They camped near a big pond.

1. The father ___fried___ eggs for breakfast.

2. In the afternoon, they _____ to an island.

3. They _____ a mountain. It started to rain.

4. They _____ back to their tent.

5. They _____ off inside the tent.

6. They _____ some games.

(After Level B, student page 99) **Constructing simple past tense; completing sentences.** Students complete
the story by looking at the appropriate illustration for that item and writing the past tense of the given verb
in the blank provided.

Write the sentences.

1. buy

They didn't buy a boat.

They bought a van.

2. see

He

3. eat

She

4. catch

It

(After Level B, student page 101) **Constructing positive and negative statements using irregular past tense verbs.** Students write a negative sentence about the picture on the left and a positive sentence about the picture on the right. Model the irregular past tense forms orally before assigning for independent work.

71

Look at the picture.
Write the missing word in the sentence.

1. drive

2. sit

3. fight

4. see

5. eat

This is what a family did on vacation last year.

1. The father ___drove___ the van. 2. His wife _____ beside him. The children sat in the back. 3. They _____ all week. 4. The family _____ penguins and fish at the aquarium. 5. The next day, they _____ lunch at a pretty beach.

(After Level B, student page 103) **Completing sentences with irregular past tense verbs.** Students complete the story by looking at the appropriate illustration for that item and writing the past tense of the given verb in the space provided.

Circle the correct word.
Write the word on the line.

1. rain

   train

   main

Pat went out in the _____rain_____ .

2. coat

   goat

   boat

We saw a _____ on the farm.

3. bed

   red

   fed
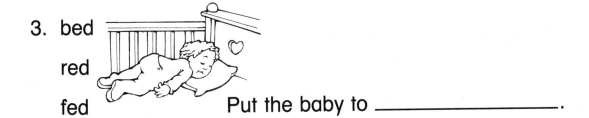
Put the baby to _____ .

4. clock

   rock

   block
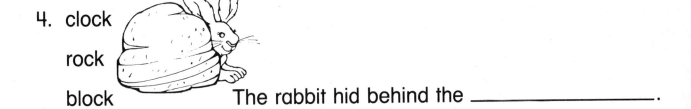
The rabbit hid behind the _____ .

5. bear

   pear

   wear
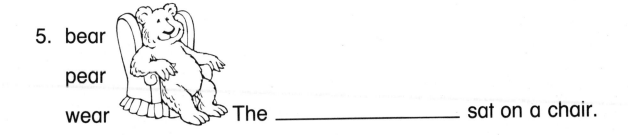
The _____ sat on a chair.

(After Level B, student page 104) **Applying phonetic decoding skills; completing sentences.** Students circle
the word that best completes the sentence and then write the word in the space provided. Encourage students
to read their completed sentences and the rhyming word choices aloud.

73

Read the story. Then read the questions.
Choose the best answer.

My name is Tina.

My Mom and Dad had a two-week vacation. We went to New York by car. It was only 200 miles, so we got there in one afternoon. The first day, we went to see the Statue of Liberty and the Empire State Building. My sister and I climbed to the top of the Statue of Liberty. That was a lot of fun!

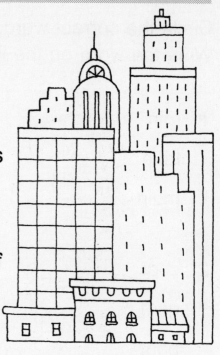

1. How did the family go to New York?

⭕ By car.

⭕ By bus.

⭕ By train.

2. How many miles was the trip?

⭕ 100 miles.

⭕ 200 miles.

⭕ 50 miles.

3. What did they see?

⭕ The World Trade Center.

⭕ The Statue of Liberty.

⭕ The Staten Island Ferry.

4. Who climbed to the top of the Statue of Liberty?

⭕ Tina and her Mom.

⭕ Tina and her Dad.

⭕ Tina and her sister.

(After Level B, student page 105) **Identifying details.** Students read the paragraph through silently and go right on to answer the questions by marking the oval next to the correct answer. Then, a volunteer reads the story aloud and other students answer the questions.

What can your magnet pull?
Check **YES** or **NO**.

		YES	NO
a penny			
paper clips			
scissors			
pencils			
a dime			
a string			
a crayon			
paper			
a jar lid			

(After Level B, student page 106) **Classifying.** Working with a partner, students test the objects listed in the chart to see if the magnet will pull them or not. They check **YES** or **NO** for each object listed. Then they add some objects of their own and test them with the magnet. They ask questions, e.g., *Can the magnet pull paper?, etc.*

Tell the math story.

1. Paul had _____ . He bought .

It cost _____ . How much did he have left? _____

2. Ann had _____ . She bought .

It cost _____ . How much did she have left? _____

3. Ed had  _____ . He bought .

It cost _____ . How much did he have left? _____

4. Jean had  _____ . She bought  .

They cost _____ . How much did she have left? _____

(After Level B, student page 106) **Math: problem solving.** Model the first problem; tell the story and have students write the amount of money and the price on the first two lines. Elicit the answer to the problem; students write 25¢ on the third line. Let students work in pairs, taking turns reading aloud and helping one another write the answers.

It was _____. It was _____ very

hard. It was very cold. The _____ were out looking

for food.

Little Rabbit _____ two turnips. He ate one. He

wanted the other turnip. But he _____ about his

_____, Little Donkey.

Little Rabbit left the turnip on Little Donkey's _____.

Little Donkey was very _____. He decided to give

the turnip to Little Sheep. He left it on her _____.

Little Sheep came _____. She decided to give the

turnip to Little Doe. She left it on her _____. Little

Doe decided to give the turnip to Little Rabbit. Rabbit was fast

_____. She left the turnip beside his _____.

Little Rabbit _____ up. He was very surprised. He

thought he was _____. He gobbled the turnip up.

dreaming	home	winter	snowing	animals
thought	asleep	friend	doorstep	woke
surprised	table	windowsill	bed	found

Circle the coins that equal each price.

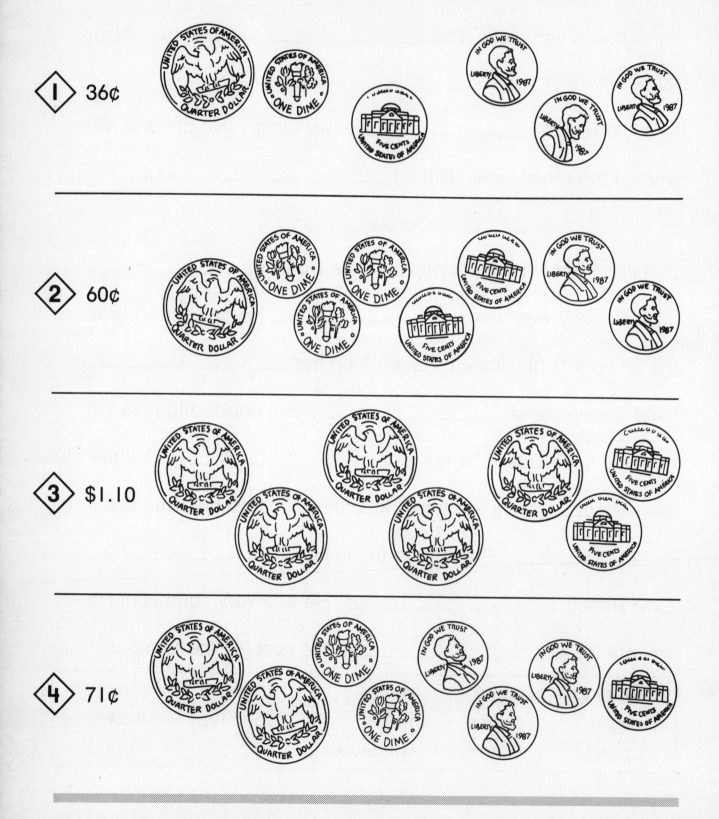

◇1◇ 36¢

◇2◇ 60¢

◇3◇ $1.10

◇4◇ 71¢

(After Level B, Unit 6) **Preparation for standardized testing: math concepts.** Students draw a circle around the group of coins that add up to the amount shown.

(After Level B, student pages 58–59, 76–77, 94–95) **Classifying.** Students follow directions on Activity Book pages 40–41, 54–55, and 66–67 to cut out art from the three sections on this page and paste it where it belongs.